W9-AUR-306

Solids, Liquids, and Gases

States of Matter and How They Change

DEVELOPED IN COOPERATION
WITH

NEW YORK HALL OF SCIENCE
CORONA, NEW YORK

No part of this publication may be reproduced in whole or in part, or stored in a retrieval system, or transmitted in any form or by any means, electronic, mechanical, photocopying, recording, or otherwise, without written permission of the publisher. For information regarding permission, write to Scholastic Inc., Instructional Publishing Group, 730 Broadway, New York, N.Y. 10003

Copyright © 1993 by Scholastic Inc.   All rights reserved. Published by Scholastic Inc.   Printed in the U.S.A.
ISBN 0-590-26136-3
2 3 4 5 6 7 8 9 10   09   99 98 97 96 95 94 93 92

THE PHYSICAL WORLD IS GOVERNED BY THE PROPERTIES AND INTERACTIONS OF MATTER AND ENERGY.

Solids, Liquids, and Gases

Matter changes in a variety of ways.

Solids, Liquids, and Gases

Read-Aloud

Matter has properties by which it can be observed and described.

Literature

Properties of matter, such as shape, color, and state, can change.

Changes in matter require adding or taking away energy.

What Did We Learn?

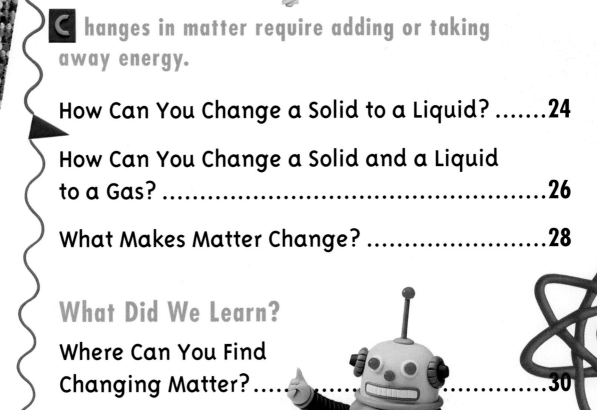

Why Does Matter Matter?

What is in the world around you?

You need:
Things from
around the room
Markers or
crayons

Go on a scavenger hunt.

❶ Find something near.
Find something clear.
And don't forget
to find something wet.
What have you found—
anything round?

❷ Draw or write what
you found.

All the things you found are matter. Matter takes up space. Everything you can see, feel, taste, or smell is matter.

THINK!
Are you made of matter?

Can You Name the Matter?

All the things you found are matter. Everything in this fish tank is matter.

Some matter keeps its shape. Will the shape of the rock change on its own?

Some matter changes shape when it pours. What shape will the water be if you pour it into a jar?

Some matter spreads out to fill the space around it. What will happen to the air bubbles?

You need:
Matter from your scavenger hunt
Containers
Balloons

Test your matter.

❶ Look at each object. What form of matter do you think it is? Is it more like the rock or the water or the air bubbles?

❷ Test your predictions. What will happen if you put it on a table, or into a new container, or into the air? ✏️

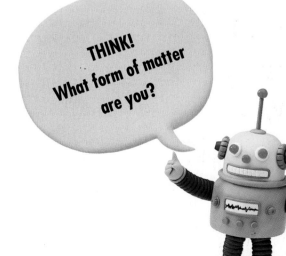

THINK!
What form of matter are you?

What Are Solids?

Some matter has a shape that you can see and feel. A solid is a form of matter that won't change shape on its own.

Could this shell change shape on its own?

Could you feel the shape of this crystal?

Take a solids walk.

1 Find the smallest solid you can see.

2 Look at it with a hand lens. Do you think it can change shape by itself?

3 Now look at a grain of salt with a hand lens. Is salt a solid? Why?

You need:
Small objects
Salt
Hand lens

THINK!
What's the biggest solid you can think of?

What Are Liquids?

Some matter has no shape of its own. A liquid is a form of matter that takes the shape of its container.

You need:
Clear containers
Beads
Water

Compare solids and liquids.

1 Pour some beads from one container into another. What happens to the shape of each bead?

2 Pour some water into a container. What shape is the water? Pour it into another container. What happens to its shape?

What would happen if you tried to pick up the puddle?

THINK!
What happens when you drop liquids?

How is the shape of the water changing?

What Are Gases?

Some matter is hard to see, but you still know it's there. A gas is a form of matter that keeps spreading out. Air is a mixture of gases.

What's inside these balloons?

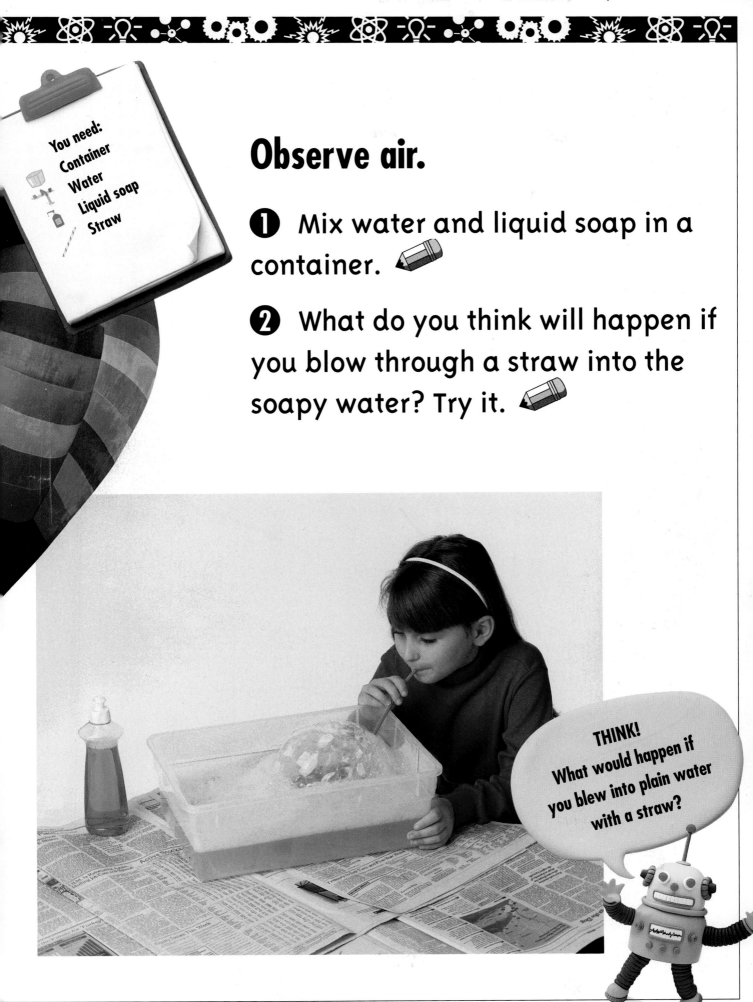

You need:
Container
Water
Liquid soap
Straw

Observe air.

1 Mix water and liquid soap in a container.

2 What do you think will happen if you blow through a straw into the soapy water? Try it.

THINK!
What would happen if you blew into plain water with a straw?

What Happens to Solids in Liquids?

Some solids float on top of liquids, and some solids sink.

What else can happen when solids and liquids are mixed together?

You need:
Plastic cups
Paper
Markers
Water
Salt
Sand
Spoons
Paper towels
Hand lens

water

Test solids in water.

1 Fill three cups with water. Put salt in one and sand in another.

2 Stir. What happens? Leave them alone for five minutes. What happens now?

3 Pour the liquids through paper towels. Look at the water. Look at the paper towels.

sand and water

water

THINK!
What would happen if you left the salt water out for a week?

What Happens to Liquids in Liquids?

You've seen solids in liquids.
What about liquids in liquids?

You need:
Jar with a lid
Water
Food coloring
Cooking oil

Mix some liquids.

❶ Add food coloring to water in a jar. Cover and shake.

❷ Add oil to your jar and cover it. What happens when you turn the jar on its side? Try it.

❸ Now shake the jar. Watch what happens. Then wait five minutes. What happens now?

Some liquids mix easily
with other liquids. Some
liquids don't mix.
Look at this picture.
Which liquids mixed?
What happened to the
liquids that didn't mix?

THINK!
What do you think will
happen if you add more
water to your jar?

What Happens to Gases in Liquids?

You've seen that air takes up space. Sometimes air takes up space inside a solid. Breathe in. What's inside your lungs?

Sometimes air takes up space in a liquid. Look at this picture. What's inside these bubbles?

You need:
Balloon
Container
Water
Safety goggles

Test gases in liquids.

1 Blow up a balloon and hold it closed. Let the balloon go. Where does the air go?

2 Blow up the balloon again and hold it under water. What happens to the water?

THINK!
How are the bubbles like the balloon?

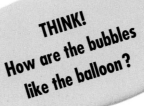

How Small Can It Get?

Solids, liquids, and gases are all made of very small parts.

You need:
Clay
Hand lens

Experiment with matter.

❶ Look at a lump of clay. How big is it? What shape is it?

❷ Break the clay in half. How big is each piece now? What shape are the pieces? Is it still clay?

❸ Break one piece in half again and again until you have the smallest piece you can make. Look with a hand lens. Is it still clay?

What if you broke your clay into smaller and smaller pieces? The pieces would be too small to see. Do you think they would still be clay?

THINK! How is a microscope like a hand lens? How is it different?

You can use microscopes to look at matter that is too small to see with your eyes.

What Is Matter Made Of?

Could you see the smallest parts of clay? All matter is made up of tiny parts that are too small to see. These parts are the building blocks of matter.

Be a building block.

❶ Some matter is solid like a rock. The building blocks are packed close together. Pretend to be the building blocks of a rock. What would you do?

❷ Some matter is liquid like water. The building blocks move around. Pretend to be the building blocks of water. How would you move?

❸ Some matter is a gas like air. The building blocks spread out. Pretend to be the building blocks of air. Where would you go?

THINK!
What if the building blocks of a gas were squeezed together?

How Can You Change a Solid to a Liquid?

Matter can change from a solid to a liquid to a gas and back again.

What will happen to the juice pop when the air warms it?

You need:
Ice cubes
Plastic bags

What will happen to the juice in the freezer?

Change a solid to a liquid.

❶ Put two ice cubes in two plastic bags. Leave one alone.

❷ Have a melting race. How can you make the other ice cube melt faster?

THINK!
What will happen if you put your melted ice cube in the freezer?

How Can You Change a Solid and a Liquid to a Gas?

Sometimes matter changes into a completely different kind of matter.

Make new matter.

You need:
Baking soda
Balloon
Spoon
Paper funnel
Vinegar
Plastic bottle

❶ Put baking soda in a balloon. Put vinegar in a bottle.

❷ Twist the balloon and put it over the bottle.

❸ Untwist the balloon and lift it so that the baking soda falls into the vinegar. What changed? What was left?

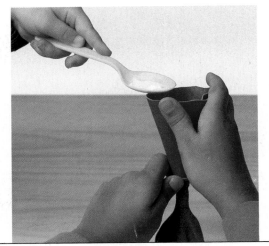

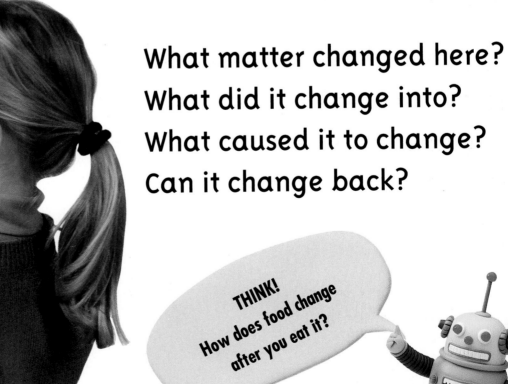

What matter changed here?
What did it change into?
What caused it to change?
Can it change back?

THINK!
How does food change after you eat it?

What Makes Matter Change?

Matter changes form when you add or take away enough heat.
What is changing form here? What is making this change happen?

Sometimes heat can make matter change to a whole new kind of matter. What could this batter change into? What will make it change?

Where Can You Find Changing Matter?

Matter is changing all around you.

You need:
Cornstarch
Water
Food coloring
Bowl

Make mystery slime.

❶ Mix cornstarch and water. Add food coloring.

❷ Let the slime run through your fingers. Do you think it's a liquid? Why? Press it into a ball. What happens?

❸ Now spread it out again. What happens? How did your slime change?

Where else can you see matter changing?

What kinds of matter could you find in the ocean?

What form of matter is ocean water?

Are there any solids in the ocean?

Do you think there are any gases in the ocean?

How is matter in the ocean changing?

Freeze: When water freezes, it gets cold enough to change from a liquid to a solid.

Gas: A gas such as air is a form of matter that spreads out to fill the space around it.

Heat: Heat is a kind of energy. Heat can change solids into liquids, and liquids into gases.

Liquid: A liquid such as water is a form of matter that changes shape when it pours. A liquid takes the shape of its container.

Matter: Everything you can see, feel, taste, or smell is matter. Everything that takes up space is matter. Solids, liquids, and gases are forms of matter.

Melt: When ice melts, it gets warm enough to change from a solid into a liquid.